Swallows
IN THE BIRDHOUSE

by **Stephen R. Swinburne**

3-dimensional watercolors by
Robin Brickman

The Millbrook Press   Brookfield, Connecticut

For Hayley and Devon, my
two little songsters.   *S.R.S.*

For my mother, Lillian,
who delights and inspires
us all.   *R.B.*

Copyright and CIP data appear
on the last page of the book

On a breezy April morning with the air full of dirt smells and the buzz of bees, Hayley and Martin watch a robin build a nest in a gnarled apple tree.

The robin has chosen a good spot. Predators can't reach the nest and the bird's home will get full sun. Soon the nest will be brimming with baby birds.

"It would be fun to build a birdhouse near our house," said Hayley.

"Great idea," answered Martin. "Let's put up a nesting box in the backyard."

Hayley and Martin pick the perfect place—a sunny spot near the vegetable garden. They take turns digging the hole for the post that the box will sit on.

The birdhouse is well built with a strong roof to keep out rain and will make a good home for a family of birds.

Now the right bird must find its new house.

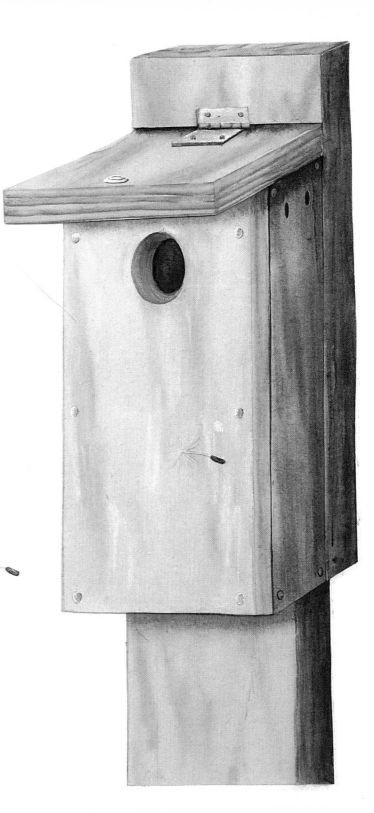

By early May, when birds sing before sunrise, the wait is over. A small bird with a moon-white breast, a dark blue-green back and narrow pointed wings circles above the box. The bird flies fast and strong and seems made of air, swerving and dipping like a leaf caught in a trick wind. It's a tree swallow. The swallow dives down to perch on the roof, looks about, and fidgets.

Hayley and Martin think their house will be the perfect home. Tree swallows are one of the easiest birds to attract to a nesting box and also one of the most common swallows in North America.

This tree swallow migrated a long way. Maybe the bird was part of a great flock of swallows from the marshes of North or South Carolina or even the coasts of Central America. Swallows winter in warm places where there are lots of flying insects to eat.

The tree swallow slips through the front hole of the birdhouse. Soon another bird swoops and glides beside the box. This is her mate, the male whose more brilliant back and wings gleam as if the sun were held in its feathers.

The two tree swallows then perch on the roof. "Weet, trit, weet, trit," they chatter, over and over again.

The female swallow flies off and returns carrying a strand of dried grass. She will do all the nest building. She stuffs the grass into the hole.

Meanwhile, the male stands ready to chase away other tree swallows. The bird spots a cat and darts above the predator, making sharp clicking calls.

The female bird continues to build the nest, flitting back and forth, back and forth, her tiny bill draped with pieces of straw, grass, pine needles, and some feathers from a nearby chicken farm.

A few days later six eggs, pure white like the swallow's breast, nestle in the cup of soft feathers and dry straw. Each egg is a little smaller than a grape. The eggs will take two weeks to develop. The female bird is a protective mother. She incubates the eggs by herself through rain and chilly weather, leaving only briefly to catch insects or to stretch her wings.

While the mother bird warms her eggs, the father bird lands nearby, preens his feathers, and twitters loud and long, over and over, announcing, "My family is coming, my family is coming!"

One bright morning at the end of two weeks, the eggs hatch. Both parents begin arriving at the box with beaks full of insects. The tree swallow nestlings lift their heads to get a view of the new world.

For the next three weeks or so, both parents become the best backyard bug catchers in the neighborhood.

Inside the box, the six nestlings grow rapidly on their insect meals eating bugs for breakfast, bugs for lunch, and bugs for dinner.

The young birds call and chatter for food. If one of the parents nears the box, the nestlings know food is coming and make a loud racket like the hiss of fast rain on a dry sidewalk.

After two weeks in the birdhouse the bodies of the young tree swallows are the size of chicken eggs. The birds wobble on shaky legs and poke their heads through the hole in the box. One nestling after another leans out with gaping, pink-yellow mouths, begging loudly for food from the busy parents.

The baby birds spend more and more time jostling to peek through the birdhouse hole. They quickly outgrow their home. On a warm afternoon, almost three weeks after hatching, a nestling squeezes out and teeters on the rim of the hole.

The baby bird flutters away from the box, wings trembling like a kite that's lost its wind. The young tree swallow's first flight is short. Once the swallows leave the birdhouse, they don't return to the box.

One parent flies to the fledgling and stuffs a flying insect into its wide mouth. Tree swallow parents will feed their young for a few days while the fledglings take bug-catching lessons.

The young birds swoop and dive about the yard, sometimes snapping up insects, sometimes missing. The young swallows soon become good at snatching their own insects in midair.

One morning a few weeks later, twenty or more tree swallows perch on the wire not far from the box in the backyard. Where did they all come from?

As the days get shorter and the nights cooler, migration begins. The family of tree swallows joins other tree swallows in preparation for their long flight south, where they will spend the winter.

One day hundreds and hundreds of tree swallows crowd the telephone wires. The birds, wing to wing, flutter up and down, animated and anxious to begin their long migration. Over the meadows and fields, huge flocks wheel and turn. The air is alive with swallow wings and swallow voices.

On a crisp Saturday morning in September,
the swallows are gone and the sky is hushed.

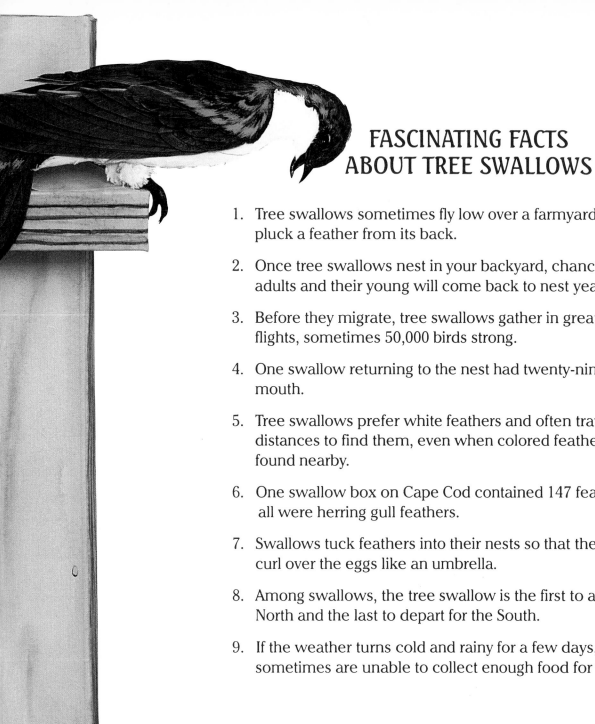

FASCINATING FACTS
ABOUT TREE SWALLOWS

1. Tree swallows sometimes fly low over a farmyard duck and pluck a feather from its back.

2. Once tree swallows nest in your backyard, chances are that the adults and their young will come back to nest year after year.

3. Before they migrate, tree swallows gather in great communal flights, sometimes 50,000 birds strong.

4. One swallow returning to the nest had twenty-nine insects in its mouth.

5. Tree swallows prefer white feathers and often travel long distances to find them, even when colored feathers can be found nearby.

6. One swallow box on Cape Cod contained 147 feathers; almost all were herring gull feathers.

7. Swallows tuck feathers into their nests so that the curved tips curl over the eggs like an umbrella.

8. Among swallows, the tree swallow is the first to arrive in the North and the last to depart for the South.

9. If the weather turns cold and rainy for a few days, swallows sometimes are unable to collect enough food for their young.

QUICK GUIDE TO
TREE SWALLOWS

SIZE: 5 to 6 inches (12 to 15 centimeters), sparrow-sized

COLOR: Adults have blue-green-black backs, white bellies; young birds have brown backs, white bellies

VOICE: "Weet, trit, weet"

DIET: Mostly flying insects, although they will eat bayberries if insects are unavailable

HABITAT: Fields and meadows, backyard gardens, forest edge, with water nearby; nests in tree holes or birdhouses

BREEDING PERIOD: April through July

NEST MATERIALS: Grass lined with feathers

NUMBER OF EGGS: 4 to 6 white eggs

INCUBATION PERIOD: 13 to 16 days by female only

NESTLING PERIOD: 16 to 24 days

FLEDGLING PERIOD: 2 to 3 days

NUMBER OF BROODS: 1

RANGE: Alaska, northern and central United States, most of Canada

HOW TO BUILD A TOP-OPENING TREE SWALLOW BIRDHOUSE

Materials

- 1 1 x 6 x 6 piece of common or white pine board ¾ of an inch (2 cm) thick
- a scrap piece of common pine or exterior plywood for roof
- 16 6-penny galvanized nails
- 1 small brass hinge
- hammer
- saw
- drill with ¼-inch (6 mm) bit
- for entrance hole, a keyhole saw or a 1½ inch (3.8 cm) bit

Procedure

1. The actual dimensions of the 1 x 1 x 6 pine board will be about ¾ inch by 5½ inches by 6 feet after planing. Saw it into the lengths indicated by the diagrams along the bottom of this page and the following one.
2. Saw ³/₈ of an inch (1 cm) off each corner of the bottom piece (to allow water to drain from the finished birdhouse).
3. Saw one edge of each of the 5½ x 9 inch side pieces off at an angle so that the front edge of each piece measures 8 inches while the back edge remains at 9 inches. (This will allow the roof to slope downward.)
4. Drill two ¼- inch holes (for ventilation) along the top (sloped edge) of each side piece.
5. Drill or saw an entrance hole about 1¹/₈ inches (2.8 cm) from the top of the front piece. It should be 1½ inches in diameter.

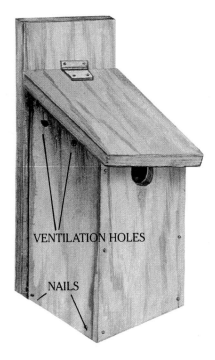

VENTILATION HOLES

NAILS

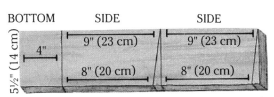

BOTTOM   SIDE   SIDE

5½" (14 cm)

4"

9" (23 cm)   9" (23 cm)

8" (20 cm)   8" (20 cm)

Cut off at a slight angle

6. On what will be the inside of the front piece, make a few shallow horizontal scratches. (This will help the nestlings to climb up and out of the box.)
7. Nail the two side pieces to the short sides of the bottom, placing two nails through each side and into the bottom where indicated in the picture on the opposite page. Be sure to place the nails at least ½ inch (1.25 cm) in from the corners.
8. Drill a 1¼ - inch hole in the center of the top of the back piece to hang the birdhouse on a tree or post.
9. Nail the front and back to the bottom, using three nails along each edge to secure the pieces to the sides as indicated at right.
10. Attach the roof with the hinge as shown.

Notes

- 2 pieces of 1 x 6 x 6 board will make 3 houses.

- If you don't have tools, ask a lumber yard or hardware store to make the cuts for you.

- If you don't have scrap wood around for the roof, ask for some at the lumber yard or a construction site. It can be anything that will not conduct cold (don't use metal) and is sturdy enough to keep the rain out. It must be at least 6½ inches by 7½ inches so that it will overhang and keep the house dry.

NAILS

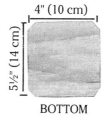

4" (10 cm)

5½" (14 cm)

BOTTOM

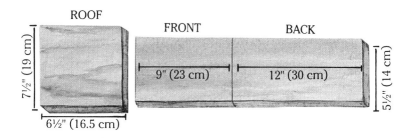

ROOF

7½" (19 cm)

6½" (16.5 cm)

FRONT

BACK

9" (23 cm)

12" (30 cm)

5½" (14 cm)

ATTRACTING TREE SWALLOWS
TO YOUR BIRDHOUSE

Buying a Birdhouse. You can buy a sturdy birdhouse for $10 or less at hardware or lawn and garden stores. Look for an unpainted wooden box, with proper ventilation and drainage and an entrance hole of 1½ inches (about 3.5 centimeters) in diameter *with no perch.* This allows a tree swallow to enter, but keeps out larger, unwanted birds such as starlings. You can stop cats and raccoons from climbing up the post by attaching a 2-foot (61-centimeter) length of thin metal flashing around the post just below the box.

Where to Put Your Birdhouse. Mount the box on a tree or post 5 to 7 feet (1.5 to 2 meters) above the ground in any open area such as a lawn, meadow, park, vacant lot, garden, or even a school playground. Tree swallows don't mind nesting near people's homes or other buildings, but they do like a clear area in front of the box so they can fly about and catch insects. Tree swallows also like to have water nearby.

When to Put Up Your Birdhouse and How Many Birdhouses to Put Up. The best time to put up your birdhouse is late winter or early spring. Tree swallows start returning in late March and early April and begin to search for a good place to nest. If you are putting up more than one birdhouse, place them from 60 to 100 feet (20 to 30 meters) apart. For instance, a meadow or lawn the size of a little league infield might hold five boxes.

Putting Out Feathers for Tree Swallows. Tree swallows dive and play with feathers anytime during their nesting cycle. But if you throw them up while they're nest building or incubating eggs, they are more likely to take them back to the box and use them in the nest. You can also leave the feathers on the ground or tie them in a string bag near the box.

Feathers can sometimes be hard to find. The best place to look is a chicken farm—or visit a local duck pond and check the shoreline for feathers. If you don't live near chickens or ducks, ask family and friends if they could spare some feathers from a down pillow. You might also see if a local craft store carries them.

Maintaining Your Birdhouse. Clean out the old nest materials after the birds have finished using the box. This prevents a buildup of mites and insects. If the birdhouse is really dirty, use mild soap and water to scrub it clean. Be sure to rinse the box thoroughly and then let it dry completely before closing it back up. Sometimes mice use the box as a cozy home for the winter, so you should also check the inside in late winter or early spring just before the birds return.

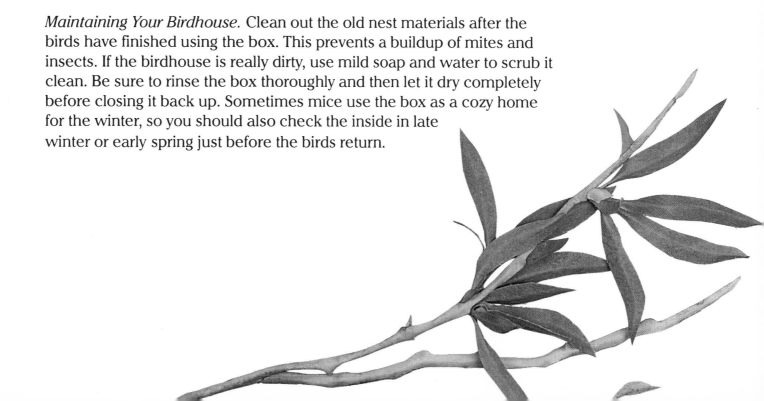

GLOSSARY

Brood—A group of young birds hatched at one time and cared for by the same parents.

Fledgling—A young bird that has left the nest and is still under the parents' care.

Incubate—To warm eggs by sitting on them so they will develop and hatch.

Migration—The movement of birds or animals from one place to another.

Nestling—A young bird still in the nest.

Predator—An animal or bird that lives by preying on, or killing, other animals.

Preen—To clean or smooth the feathers with the beak or bill.

A note about the art: These illustrations are watercolors that have been cut, sculpted, and glued together to form three-dimensional sculptures. The illustrator would like to thank Howie Levitz of TGL Photo for his skillful photography, Heather Williams and Colin Orians for biological expertise, and Jeff, Jared, and Caleb for their immense help during the creation of the art.

The author wishes to thank Chris Rimmer of the Vermont Institute of Natural Science and Laura Backes of the Children's Book Insider.

Library of Congress Cataloging-in-Publication Data
Swinburne, Stephen R.
Swallows in the birdhouse / by Stephen Swinburne; illustrated by Robin Brickman.
p. cm.
Summary: Two children put up a birdhouse in their backyard and watch as a pair of tree swallows build a nest and raise six babies before migrating south in the fall. Includes information about tree swallows and about birdhouses.
ISBN 1-56294-182-8
1. Tree swallow—Juvenile literature. [1. Tree swallow. 2. Swallows. 3. Birdhouses.] I. Brickman, Robin, ill. II. Title.
QL696.P247S95   1996   598.8'13—dc20   95-9500   CIP   AC